ISBN 978-1-913185-02-2

Published by Stan's Cafe
Birmingham, UK
2019

www.stanscafe.co.uk

Ocean of Storms

So Bring Me Down

Space Station

**A stage play, a radio play and
a durational performance
by Stan's Cafe**

Contents

OCEAN OF STORMS

Two figures arrive on a raised metal mesh floor, for convenience we call them Angels. Beneath this floor, as will be revealed, lies earth and on the earth a string of blue festoon bulbs which, on occasion, pretend to be stars. The Angels bring with them two silver flight cases, one of which contains tea making equipment, the other a model Earth that works as a reference point or possibly a monitor onto the planet's surface.

It is gradually surmised that the Angels are on a mission to find a small girl who is lost in a city. They attempt to track this girl through the world's telephone and radio conversions. Their mission is disrupted when they pick up Jo, an astronaut in distress. The Angels attempt to bring the astronaut home by voicing mission control, raising the floor, stepping on the earth and moving the landing lights.

With the floor replaced and landing lights now stars rearranged in the sky the girl is found. She is possibly boarding a bus for home and Jo starts a hazardous reentry as other familiar lost voices all start to turn for 'home'.

The Angels do not have names, they are identified here with the initials of the original performers. Section headings are purely for rehearsal purposes.

The Voices.

[After arriving and setting up cases]

S   We've got your jumper here for you, yes, brown cashmere, it'll be ready for pick up on Thursday. Do you want extra salami on that, any garlic bread?

Hello my name's Charlotte, I'm calling from Panes Plus. I wonder, do you have time to answer some questions for me?

Do you live on a busy main road?

A   I'm sorry the number you have dialled has not been recognised.

Hello I'm just calling to say thank you for a wonderful and I mean wonderful night, we must do it again some time.

My name's Maxine and what can I do for you? I'm twenty one, genuine blonde and 36, 24, 36. I'm lying on my bed at the moment and I've taken off all my clothes.

S   Hello Gran how are you?

A   And I'm feeling so hot.

S   Are you? That's nice.

A   Now we can get down to something really serious.

Hello Jerry?

S   Yes.

A   I've done it for yer.

S   Oh lovely lovely.

A   It's yer alternator.

S   Yes black and white ones.

A   An' I've done yer oil switch an' all.

S   How many kittens have you got left?

A   That'll cost you 80 quid.

S   Oh, I didn't think it would be that much!
A   When are yer going to pick it up mate?
S   I'll be round to see them on Thursday.
A   Hello Mr.Thompson, this is Joan.
S   No.
A   I've got your Bobby here.
S   No.
A   He's been in our garden again.
S   No, no that can't be true.
A   That's the third time this week.
S   No, no you must have made a mistake.
A   No, you see we only stock the short ones not the long ones, you must have got the wrong manufacturer.
S   I'm afraid that line's busy at the moment can you hold?
A   Can you call me back? It's urgent.

S   No I'm afraid that line's busy.

A   It doesn't matter when, I'll stay up.
S   Putting you on hold.
A   I'll wait...
S   I can't speak to you now.
A   .... that's all.
        I didn't mean it.
S   I'd like to complain about my perm, I only had it done last week and it's falling out already, it's a disaster.
A   And with the VAT that's going to bring it up to £24.50.
S   Yeah POB, approaching number 74, then I've got a pick up at...

A   Bonjour, bonjour Monsieur.
S   Hello.
A   Er avez vous une chambre?
S   Yes.
A   Une chambre?
S   Yes, it's at the end of the corridor.
A   Pour deux personne?
S   It's got a sink in it but you've got to share a
        bathroom.
A   Ce combien?
S   It's about £45 per week.
A   Ah.
S   Are you a single woman?
A   Non, non.
S   I'm sorry, we only rent to single women.
A   Ah merci beaucoup Monsieur.
S   I'm sorry, bye bye.

A   Suzie are you there? Come on pick up the phone
        Suzie.
S   I'm sorry we don't deal with emergencies.
A   Come on pick up the phone.
S   I'm sorry we don't deal with emergencies.
A   I know you're there.
S   You'll have to try our other number, treble 2
        treble 4.
A   I just want to talk to you.
S   I'm sorry.
A   Have it your own way.
S   Yes, I'd like to speak to the manager. Yes, it's my
        washing machine, it's burning all my clothes.
A   Can't get it started. Volkswagen Polo, 1983.
        Oh yeah 345, 346, 856.

How long will you be?
S   About twenty minutes.
A   Oh great!
S   I'm at the service station.
A   Ruskin Street.
S   I'm just going to have something to eat, then I'll
        be on my way.
A   Okay, I'll wait by my car.

A   Yeah, I'm at the hospital.
S   Hello.
A   Don't panic, but I've written the car off.
S   Do you want to speak to my mum?
A   No, I'm fine, it's just that Harry's got to stay in.
S   Only she's not here right now.
A   This is important. Go up to Harry's bedroom.
S   She's gone out.
A   We've got to find out what the tablets are on his
        bedside table.
S   She'll be back in about an hour.
A   No, go to Harry's bedroom. Get his tablets.
S   Do you want me to take a message?
A   We've got to know what they are or they can't
        give him an anaesthetic.
S   She's gone to Tesco.
A   He's lost a lot of blood and they've got to take
        him into theatre and we've got to know what his
        tablets are.
S   She'll be back in about an hour.
A   Just do it!
S   What's your name? My name's Angela.

S		No, we're having a great time. No, the weather is wonderful. It's great! Send you a postcard.

A		...not here at the moment but if you leave your name and number we'll...

S		I'd like to place an advert. No, it's my husband.

A		What? Of course I was asleep, its four in the morning!

S		Is Maria there?

A		I don't want to talk about this now.

S		Oh, she's on lates.

A		I'll call you in the morning okay.

S		Okay.

S		I've tried you at home, I've tried you on your mobile.

A		Why can't you come back? Oh not again! This isn't fair on the kids you know.

S		Oh, you're still not in.

A		How's mum?

S		No, she said she was going to meet me here.

A		Give her my love.

S		No, about nine.

A		So I'll see you next week.

S		No, we were going down the pub.

A		Sorry the doctor isn't here at the moment, can I help?

S		Yes, I'd like you to play a record for my husband. He's been working away from from home for about three weeks. We like to listen to Elvis together. Yes, *Love Me Tender*.

S		They haven't lived here for ages.

A   Jamie, is that you? Thank God! Well, where are you? Jamie, we've been worried sick.
        Well, why don't you come back? We'll come and get you. Do you have a phone number? Jamie, I don't understand, what did we do?

Sarah's first bus text.

        [At Globe in box]

S: Blast off. 15.50: Vicarage Road, the All Electric Garages, Curl Up & Dye Hair. Over railway, skip lorry hazards and flashing headlights. Calthorpe Arms and the ubiquitous Wood Lane. Road still curving right, 5060B Reservoir Road Surgery. A cafe with beige chairs (plastic). A Safeways bag. New Sainsbury, big bus queue and a mass of cars. Two ladders on an Astra estate. A satellite dish stares at the sky. Brian Emery. Vivian Road and St. Peter's Road. Tiny little outhouses. 14.40: yellow hatch zone 14.41: now the canal double width below. 14.50: Aberdeen Street, Norman Street, Lodge Road, Preston Road.

A   Hello operator....I think I'm having a problem with my phone. I've not had any calls for about 36 hours or so.

S   Hello Mrs Wilson? I'm phoning from Churchfields Primary School. I was just wondering, why hasn't Tony been in?
        Oh he is is he? Well next time could you write a sick note?

A   Hello Becky. It's me. I'm in London. I just got on a train didn't I. No I didn't pay. Oh God Becky its brilliant you've got to come down! I've met this bloke. Ed, oh he's really fantastic right, he's got this flat in Brixton, we're all staying there its really brilliant you've got to come down.

S   No I haven't got my bus fare.
A   What did they say?
S   No, I can't come home.
A   It's none of your business.
S   It's getting dark.
A   I don't care.
S   Can you come and get me?
A   I don't like it here.
S   What?
A   Can I come home?
S   We said twelve o'clock.
A   Please.
S   What do you think you're doing?
A   I don't like anyone.

S   We've been waiting up.
A   Can you come and get me?
S   Your father's called the police.
A   I want to come back.
S   Have you been drinking?
A   Dad we've run out of money, can you send us
        thirty quid?
S   No I'm sorry we haven't had any sightings.
        You're going to have to repeat the description.
A   This is Mrs Collins. That's right, Elaine Collins.
        Well, um you'll think I'm being really silly but
        Rachel went out on her bike to the shops about
        an hour and a half ago and she hasn't come back.
        Yes, I've phoned her, she's not there.
        Oh, I can't remember now it's silly isn't it. A red
        anorak. I think she's wearing a red anorak and
        jeans and trainers. I appreciate that, thank you.
S   We just thought you aught to know, Sam wasn't
        on the swimming coach tonight.
A   Yeah, we've got her, she's pretty jet lagged.
S   No, I've got to work late, you pick her up.
S   No, I'm in a terrible state, it's my washing
        machine it's...
A   What, is that you?
S   I can't get the money in.
A   I can't her you.
S   I can't get the money in.
A   It's a very bad line.
S   Hold on hold...
A   Don't hang up.
S   Hold on the beeps are going to go.
A   Don't hang up.
S   Hold on!

A   I'll be home in about thirty minutes.
         23.01 and the next one after that's...

Surveillance.

S   Sam. Over by Classical. Do you see her? Blue
         jacket, black shoulder bag. Got her? Keep an
         eye, yep she's been hanging around for hours.
         She's moving toward Easy Listening now, no keep
         an eye on that bag. I don't know, just keep an
         eye.
A   I'm at the station can you come and get me?
S   I've got her. Yeah, black bag just turned into
         Navigation Street. She's with a man. Tall, fair hair.
         Is he? No, he's not with her. No, she's turned into
         the station.
A   Yeah yeah, she's moving south fast, we've got
         her. White Escort registration Sierra 311 Delta
         Tango Foxtrot. George Road turning east.
         St.James's Road, she's jumped the lights.
S   She's entering the building now, black coat, red
         shoulder bag, she's looking around, she suspects
         something.
A   She doesn't suspect anything we're right up
         behind her, she's on Level 4. Blue jeans, red
         jumper, plastic bag.
S   Blond hair, sunglasses, she's looking at her watch.
         Do you recognise her?
A   No, she's not moved at all, she's waiting for
         someone.
S   Blond hair, black skirt, bare legs yep, corner of
         Bradford Street and Broom Street.
A   I've got her I think, dark hair five four. I don't
         know, yeah yeah it's her, I'm going after her.

S   Stay where you are she's on camera leaving the toilets. She's changed her jacket, wait for my word.

A   She's getting in a cab Charlotte Road, turning into Wellington Road, Belview, you've lost her.

S   No no I've got her, she's got a parcel, it's her, she's put her hood up.

A   Get a shift on she's approaching the house.

S   There's an alarm on Level 3, far end. Yep someone's opened the fire exit. You take it.

A   Negative stay where you are she's coming your way, repeat your way stick tight.

S   Speedwells Road, Alexandra Road, you're going to loose her.

A   As per the plan, she's all yours.

S   I've got her, confirm Ridley Street, Gough Street, silver puffer jacket, she's running.

A   She's all yours.

S   Any second now, the train's pulling in, repeat the description, over.

A   Five ten, mid-twenties, shoulder length dark hair, last seen...

S   She's dyed her hair and lost weight but it's definitely her, she's turning into Hooper Street it's a cul-de-sac, we've got her. No no we've lost her, repeat, we've lost her. No, it's not her.

A   Okay Mrs Collins can you give us a description of what Rachel was wearing?
        Okay right that's not very much to go on, can you be more specific than that?

S   Just leave it.

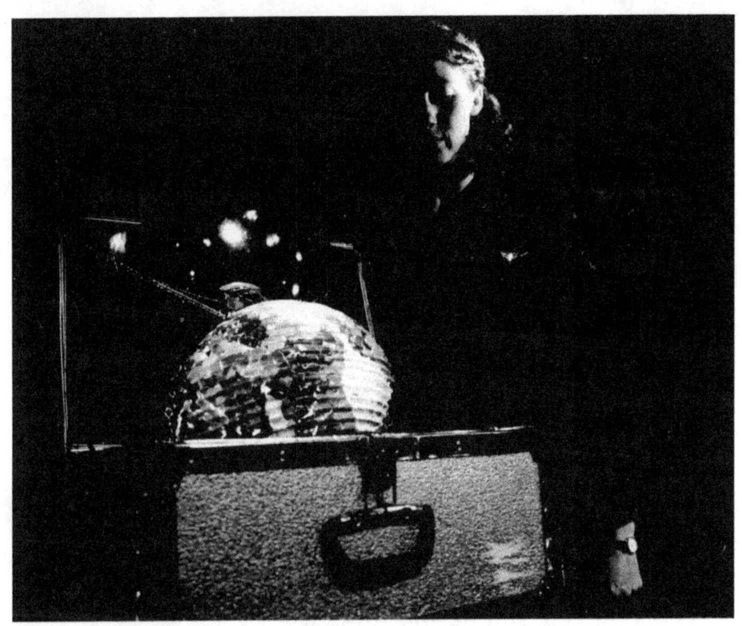

Amanda's bus text.

      [At Globe]

A   George Dixon School, bushes concealing houses.
Elmtree Road. Sold, For Sale, For Sale.
Abandoned Girls School, A457 and Hospital.
Birds nest atop a bare tree, like a cancer in the
top branches. Litter scatters up the hill. I'm
thirsty. Trafalgar Road, could be anywhere.
Scrubland, terraces. Alfred Road, Britain. New
fake old furniture. Flake paint window sill.
Window too dirty to see through.

S   Hello Caroline?

A   Total mystery land now.

S   Yeah its me.

A   47.

S   I just wondered...

A   48 on the lamp posts.

S   Can you come over?

A   50.

S   Only, I've got something to tell you. No, it's important you've got to come over. No, I can't tell you on the phone. It's just really stupid that's all. No, just really dumb. I've taken a lot of pills Caroline.

A   Broken sign.

S   Oh I don't know, too many.

A   Alfred Road.

S   About an hour ago, only, I don't feel so good now. No, I'm beginning to feel a bit sick, dizzy. Will you come over?

A   Hello Service Control, how can we help you?

S   Only I wish I hadn't done it now.

A   That shouldn't be a problem at all.

S   I feel dizzy.

A   We should have some one with you within thirty minutes.

S   Can you come over?

A   You're welcome.

S   Oh, bye.
        Lateral burn completed and I'm standing over the Indian Ocean. Everything is going as per the book. Is it against regulations to enjoy yourself this much on duty? Roger CapCom.

A   We should move onto Experiment Four now.

S   Will you want anything else from me Al?

A   You look good from here. Great, you should take a look outside.

S   Don't worry about me Al, it's nice up here, I'm

very happy.

A   Okay CapCom, I might just do that.

S   We've got that SP1 alarm flashing orange again.

A   Are you going to require further stats? Do you
     want me to standby here?
     Standing by. Okay Al, I'm sitting tight.

S   Just sit tight, your father and I will pick you up as
     soon as we can.

A   55.Zero1 55.Zero 2.

S   Kelly! How are you? Where are you? How did you
     get there? Where are you staying Kelly? Oh
     what's his name? When are you coming back?
     What about your mum Kelly, your exams?

S   CapCom this is Ocean Rider do your read me?
     Come in cap com this is ocean rider come in Al
     do you read me Al?

A   Welcome to *The Late Show* and if you've just
     joined us here, we've got a caller on Line 3.
     What's your name?

S   Hello CapCom, this is Ocean Rider.

A   ...and do you have a message for anyone out
     there tonight?

S   It's cold up here.

A   That's really beautiful Andrew and if you're
     listening out there, she loves you very much.

S   I'm loosing power.

A   Do you have any requests?

S   I need a guidance report urgently.

A   Well we'll see what we can do and meanwhile if
     there's anyone out there with a special message
     then call us now on 224 2000.

S   Ocean Rider to CapCom, I'm loosing you, come
     in Al.

A   Jo, we're going to need a guidance report at this
        time. Give us your status altitude and location.
        Fire away Jo. 5.04: check 5.02: check. Okay Jo
        we're going to take a secondary on those stats.
        Do you read me on that Jo? Ah, Ocean Rider do
        you copy on that?
S   L & C Al.
A   Jo, at this time we are a little concerned about
        your location. You're looking slightly off from
        down here. We'd like you to initiate an
        adjustment firing.
S   Sorry Al, must have taken a wrong turn back
        there.
A   That's okay Jo, we'll get you and the baby back
        on course.
S   Are you wanting to do that from down there?
A   Negative, we're recommending going local down
        here.
S   That's fine if you trust my driving.
A   There's none better Jo. It's recommended that
        you take some food on board at this time. That's
        an order.
S   Hello Carol?
A   I don't want any mistakes.
S   Yes I know.
A   It's a long ride home.
S   Mmm I just got back from Lynn's.
A   Do you want any messages?
S   No, it's bad news.
A   Just the usual.
S   Yes, their little boy ran off again.
A   We're going to initiate an adjustment firing.
        Mark 30 seconds and we're go.

	You have local and manual fire.
S	That's affirmative.
A	Ready for settings.
S	Ready for settings.
A	22 to 32.
S	22 to 32.
A	24 to 21.
S	24 to 21.
A	12 to zero 9.
S	12 to zero 9.
A	Standing by for a 6 second burst.
S	Standing by.
A	Hold her steady now Jo. And engines off. Jo, Bill's come through to us on those stats and it's confirmed there's a progressive discrepancy.
S	Yes.
A	Looks like you and the bird are in a decaying orbit.
S	Yes, it's black lambs wool.
A	Okay we've got everyone on line working on those right now Jo.
S	It was about last Thursday.
A	We're going to do all we can to keep you out there but uhh.
S	Will you have a look for me?
A	Otherwise we just want you back S & S.
S	I appreciate that. Okay Al approaching QT time. Is there anything else you want from me? Any jobs?
A	Negative you get yourself some R&R.
S	I'll prepare to go radio silence speak to you in forty.
A	Roger Ocean Rider and out.

Jo Sleeping.

A 15.27

S: This is your constellation.
   These lights are cities floating in the black.
   I'm still, these lights are moving past me.

A The North Star Pub – pill box with a porch.

S You must be tired Al.

A Bill Doyle in orange.

S This is my favourite time.

A Graveyard.

S When I can hear you but you're saying nothing.

A Shard End Glass.

S When the earth has disappeared and there are
   just star lights and city lights.
   I'm the earth and those city lights are floating in
   the heavens.

A   Check.
S   And you're looking down on me and I'm looking
        up at you.
        And I cradle your light in my eye.
A   Check.
S   And I'm still and they're moving.
        And I play the Early Bird Angel.
A   Check.
S   And the stars could be the cities and the cities
        could be the stars.
        and they have all become serene.
A   Satellite dish.
S   I can hear you sleeping on in the sky and the
        darkness.
A   Check.
        Photographic land and nitrate soil.
A   20 yards ahead.
S   I can hear your breathing.
        I bring it in into my lungs.
A   Okay.
S   The storms are outside.
        The ocean and the rest.
A   A fixed distance.
S   These are the last instants of nothing.
        Golden frequency rain.
A   Lighting striking.
        A retina dance.
S   Scars on the station.
        Land lines.
        Trunk route.
        Numbers.
A   Sensitisation of earth.
        Telegraph muscle.

Radiation.
Digital meteors burning the sky.
S   Check.
A   Blitzkrieg on retinal land.
        Liquid sky, ionised path.
S   The lightning field.
A   Corpse grass.
        The ash museum.
        Lost sights never fading.
S   15.39: duffle coat, hood up and shades.
A   Let me float away, watch from out here.
S   A man hitches up his trousers.
A   Here comes the sun and with it the Earth is
        fading into being.
        Those are the stars, cities are disappearing.
        Here comes the land and the sea.
S   Check.
A   Nature has taken over again.
S   The fifty mile estimate begins to look good.
A   Check.
        Your breathing is disappearing in a static crackle
        You go with the night and the city stars
        You've gone. I'm beyond the sky.
S   Engine off again.
A   I can look but not touch.
S   She's looking good.
A   I'm flying so fast.
        No one can touch me.
S   All over this route letters are missing from signs.
        Somewhere they are reassembled to spell out a
        stolen message.
A   16.16
S   You're there, somewhere.

Young woman, bare legs. She's playing ball with
A thin strip of a lad, not her.

Sarah's second bus text.

[at Globe]

S This is nearer Gravelly Hill. Lamp post 46, shelter
505949D. Flying duel carriageway style,
Chevrolet parked on a drive (passing America).
Beige taxi satellite. Prospect Vehicle Sales. Cable
pavement scars are fading. Light that warns of
speeding. That chimney, this junction. A glimpse
of trace of parallel yellow lines. Mother and
daughter. Three life belts on that island in the
pond. Billesley. Kids on a roundabout, one girl in
a silver jacket, maybe it's her. Someone has a
radio on quietly, DJ tones. Budding trees west of
town again. 917 is a night bus.

Home Text.

A Come in Ocean Rider.
Come in Ocean Rider.
Ocean Rider this is CapCom do you read me?
Come in.
Come in.
Closer to the touch down zone.
She's escaping mum.
She's leaving you.
Draw this in, make it closer, closer.
We make this a coming down place.
We make this a touching down scene for the
distant ones.
She's cleared the road, the corner, the place we
came from.

She's escaping your gravity.
She's just a speck now, rubbed out by the street
lights and sweep of headlights passing through
the rain.
Stubble gun land spreading itself.
Stirchley sign.
Floodlights over parkland pointing upwards,
lighting the sky.
Far voice, distant speech and stretched out voice.
Slowly, gently now, like the most delicate touch
you can imagine, gently.
Trace that line down, just brushing the thinnest
hairs breadth whisper of a distance and hold it
there.
Glasses on the top of a bus shelter.
I'm thirsty.
Compressed air hush.
Hold it there, don't take it any closer.
You're too far away now.
Come in, come in, that's it.
Now, with the most untouchable touch,
humming distance held.
You can reach out now. Just reach out now.
With just one movement and you can lift the
whole thing clear out,
and three two one.
The whole enormous unspeakable thing,
just there, in your hand with you turning it all.
You're miles high.
Effortless.
Camera eye.
Night silence sliding on.
Turning by, passing by.

Frictionless, sealed off.
Perfectly smooth, circling round.
Going going...
It's going fine Mum, I'm having a great time!
5T Zone Ends. City Centre 3 miles.
Lost altitude. Big junction. Yellow hazard zone.
New Look on the side of a lorry.
It's fantastic, I don't miss home at all!

Memory #1.
[Steam has been coming from the kettle.
Amanda's Home Text as described Sarah making
two mugs of tea. Now radio microphones and
the soundtrack are off while they drink]

S I'm saying goodbye to my mother and I don't
know what to do. I don't know where to put my
feet. I just want to be away and to kiss goodbye.
As I leave the door her hand touches my
shoulder, a double impact. It could be patting, as
you pat a dog or a disconsolate team-mate.
Maybe she was just brushing two flecks of fluff
from my jacket.
As I drive away from home I think about how that
place will always be the sun so long as I live
within its orbit. If I live here, away and bare no
thoughts of home then yes, this here, this will be
my sun and I will be my own room's satellite.

Memory #2.

A   My grandmother has been away from home. She is surrounded by her closest relations, three children, three grandchildren, she is lost. She wants to go upstairs to the room in which she spent the night, but that is now two hours drive away. She does not know where she is. She is polite, decorous, lost. She shakes my hand, kisses her son, but when she sees her daughter, there is a coming home hug and she holds, and she holds. A docking-bay clasp, back to the daughter-ship. "Are we going home now?" she asks "Yes".

S   Al, I don't care what the boys say, I want you to bring me home.
I'll take my chances.
No it's my choice.
I don't belong here any more.

Al, I don't want to die out here.

A   This is Institution Road.

S   No, its pretty fucked up here Al.

There's a bush fire and... it looks beautiful.

A   White flints cast in dark soil.

S   There's a storm, and those people and...

A   Rain drenched windows.

S   I miss you Al.

A   Traffic lights diffracted in water pools.

S   And there's my little girl.

A   She holds up an umbrella for the rain protection and a forearm obscures her face. It's her!

S   Check.

A   She's there in that scatter of sodium orange.

S   Check.

A   Standing by a bus stop, she's crying.

S   Check.

A   Don't let them touch her.

S   Roger.

CapCom do you read me?

A   Go ahead Jo.

S   I wasn't joking Al.

A   What?

S   I want you to bring me back.

A   Negative. Risk assessment says no go Jo. Just sit tight.

S   I'm cold Al.

A   I understand.

Jo?

S   I don't belong up here, Al.

A   We daren't bring you back Jo.

S   I want a chance to hold my girl again.

A   She sees a bus coming.

S   Low slung sky line, industrial spaces. A helicopter
        hovers.
A   It's too risky Jo.
S   She's searching in her pockets for the fare.
A   Jo, just sit tight.
S   I'm going with Brown 6a (19 96) customised.
A   She wears a silver jacket.
        Pockets and paper-shred tissues.
S   Reading down with K codes: 53, 57, 11, 48 and
        352L.
A   Okay Jo, I don't want you going crazy out there,
        let me get some figures together.
S   I'm reading them off now Al.
A   Hold on Jo that's 53, 57, 11.
S   48 and 352L, I'm skipping to P11.
A   P11 let's see, that's readings on tables LR+B to D.
S   Check.
        Check.
        Check.
A   Mascara.
S   Check.
A   Silver coin in a dirty hand.
S   Check.
A   Splashes in a puddle.
S   That's all systems bar SSP, DA and NIC one
        hundred PC.
        That's set, looks like we're all set.
A   Watch dial under street lamp.
S   Stand by to initiate reentry.
        Next time round I'm coming in ready or not,
        do you have any settings for me?
A   We read you Ocean Rider, ah give us a few
        seconds.

Jo, I want you to prepare to use the Emergency
Code, that's on Card 3.
The current code is 376L until we advise you
otherwise, stand by for further instructions.
[Lift floor]

A   Okay Ocean Rider we've been looking at the
         telemetry projections and it looks like we're
         going to bring you down in the Green Zone. It's
         daylight there, sea conditions are good. We'll
         have a patrol looking out for you. There's a bunch
         S32s and they estimate pick up time at sixty that's
         six zero minutes after splash down.

S   Ah we recommend you change setting PIW to 38
         yellow. How's it looking up there Jo?

A   Listen ah, Bill's here and he says you're clear to
         detach Part Two from Part One. Engine locks off.
         Ready to go local. Switch it to manual fire. That's
         all primary and intermediary stages completed,
         she's all yours. ETTM three minutes. We'll get her
         home Jo don't worry, just wait on our mark.
         [Move bulbs]

S	A route full of Saint's names, rebuilding the tower blocks.
A	Fake leather coat, fly poster bins.
S	Wellington Road.
A	She's there.
S	For sale, For Sale, For Sale, Sold.
A	50p to anywhere in town.
S	Left turn, Co-Op travel, Vivian Road.
A	Check those readings. Frank can we lock the doors in here?
S	Petrol, Cat Show, Lodge Road.
A	Old man, cracked tooth smile. She's looking good Jo.
S	Preston Road.
A	Bud I want you to bypass all the fuses to everything. We're all set.

S   Fork in the road, Town Centre two miles, she's
         climbing aboard.
A   Engine turning, waiting.
S   Al, are you still there?
A   I'm not getting anything?
S   Al?
A   Come in Ocean Rider, do you read me?
S   Do you read me?
A   Jo?
S   How long now?
A   Not long, you look great from down here Jo.
         Everyone's very happy. All systems read as
         normal. The Uncle is happy, Bill's happy, we're all
         super relaxed down here.
S   Likewise Al. How long?
A   We have one minute before the mark Jo. You're
         strapped in?
S   None tighter.
A   That's good. It's all looking good. We're all
         looking forward to seeing you again.
         Fifteen.
S   Compressed air hush.
A   Let's make it a safe one.
S   Yellow light blinking.
A   Stand by for 10 seconds of manual fire.
A   Five, four, three, two, one, mark and...
S   Engine growl.
A   2,3,4,5 the fall has started.
         [floor back]
S   Instrumentation says the fall is good. Navigation
         is green.
A   Check.
S   There's no stopping me now Al, I'm coming

home.

A   Roger Jo we're all looking out for you.

S   You should get yourself outside Al and watch me barrel on in.

A   Negative Jo, estimate 90, nine zero seconds to radio white out, I'm sticking with you.

S   Appreciated CapCom, we have cabin pressure holding at 5.5, E&I temperatures rising fast. All remaining systems remain go. We're falling fast Al, hope they welded this one tight.

Return Calls.

[all on tape]

S   Yeah I've been looking into the train times, well there's one at 11.15 and one at 1.30. Yeah but if I get the 1.30 I have to wait about an hour. No, no it'll be all right. Okay, I'll see you tomorrow.

A   I'm in the city centre, yeah all right then I'll get a bus. No, no it's not a problem see you in about half an hour. All right bye.

S   Yeah yeah I'll meet you at the Town Hall then, bye.

A   Hello? Okay I'll just put you through.

S   Yeah about 20 minutes love, ah ha.

A   I'm so pleased you called!

S   Yeah I'm just getting off the train now.

A   Are you all right?

S   Put the dinner on.

A   Oh was the weather terrible? Oh dear, all right then okay, fine, bye.

S   Yeah, I just thought you'd like to know; Andrew woke up this morning. About 5am. Yes, we've moved him onto the main ward.

S	Yeah, yeah he's on his way, yeah about five minutes. I'll get him to toot when he's outside.
A	Customs have been really good about it actually. Paperwork, just loads of paperwork, hopefully we should get the body back in the country next Tuesday.
S	Yeah he is yeah, I'll just give him a shout.
A	I got your message, oh no, no you did the right thing, definitely.
S	Oh, he isn't that's a shame, never mind, get him to give me a call when he gets in.
A	Just, just stay there. I'm coming over now. No I don't mind, just stay there. I'll be about 10 minutes.
S	Yeah Angela said you called, she's getting ever so good at taking messages.
A	Hello, Mrs.Collins, good news I think, we've had a sighting of someone fitting Rachel's description. Birmingham. Of course, were working on it right now, we'll let you know as soon as we know anything.
S	Hello, you've had me on hold, extension 2 double 9.

End Text.

[A tiny spot of light approaches the globe - live voices]

A: Under the grand circles, magnetic loops and guidance stars.
A face held up to the sky, gazing.
Jagged lightning traceries of blood across the white. An earth with blurred circumference.
Dark peat land ploughed for the rain of light,

reflections off the face of a potassium white
streak hurtling in.

S: She'll be on her way now Mum, a flaming fireball
barrelling out of the sky.

She's heading home now Mum, starting to burn,
shaking and her blood's gone heavy. Is that heat I
can feel coming through? This window's leaking
and I can barely read my watch in this bouncing.
A sign storms round so fast its just one flickering
word and the nose-cone, its going white hot.

A: She's probably walking now, out of some dense
black billowing oil smoke, helmet under her arm,
saluting the flag, kissing the children, smiling
from behind her sunglasses, she could be a hero
by now Mum.

Have you got a radio? Can we listen to it, right at
the end of the dial? I like to listen to the space
talk as I fall asleep. Do you ever do that? Right
out there at the high end of the dial, with the
static and the bleeps and the astronauts.

[Angels pack up and leave]

Original Programme Notes

Stan's Cafe
OCEAN OF STORMS

Devised and performed by
Sarah Dawson – Amanda Hadingue
with direction and texts by James Yarker

Soundtrack created by Webster West Ink
Set by Stan's Cafe and Simon Attwood
Lighting by Paul Arvidson and Stan's Cafe

Ocean of Storms won a Barclays New Stages Award and
was made with the additional financial support of:
The Arts Council Of England,
West Midlands Arts and Birmingham City Council

Ocean of Storms was first performed at mac,
Birmingham June 1996

A Note On Authorship
The authorship of devised works is always shared. *Ocean
of Storms* is no exception. The text was built from
material worked in a variety of ways with its origins either
in written scripts or improvisations.

"Have you got a radio? Can we listen to it, right at the
end of the dial? I like to listen to the space talk as I fall
asleep. Do you ever do that? Right out there at the high
end of the dial with the static and the bleeps and the
astronauts."

So Bring Me Down

So Bring Me Down was commissioned by NOW 98, Nottingham's annual performance festival, for their radio station NOWFM.

Spread over the six days of the radio station's licence these short programmes, many of them only 30 seconds long, combined to tell the astronaut story from *Ocean of Storms*. Scattered unannounced through the station's schedule the central conceit was that the NOWFM frequency was occasionally shared by Jo, an astronaut lost in space and contemplating a suicidal attempt at re-entry into the Earth's atmosphere and Al, her mission controller. Working in a fake 'real time' these programmes worked as their own trailers, building towards Jo's attempt to return home.

The joy of being commissioned by an experimental station was a freedom to play not just with scheduling, but with static, silence, distortion and unpredictability. A year or after *So Bring Me Down* archive recordings of the first Apollo moon landing were broadcast by the BBC in a similar fake 'real time'.

Jo – Sarah Dawson
Al – Amanda Hadingue
Text / Direction – James Yarker
Production – Brian Duffy & Jony Easterby
Music – Duffy & Easterby
Additional Music – Richard Chew.

Commissioned by: Andrew Chetty for Now98

Tuesday #1 16:05 (30 Secs)

J Come in?
   Do you read me?
   You're there Al, come on.
   I'm here. I'm not going anywhere.
   Please call.
   It's okay.
   Please.

Tuesday #2 15:11 (30 Secs)

J Do you read me?
A Hello.
J Hello, do you read me?
A Do you want to speak to my mum?
J Sorry Al?
A She's not here.
J I need some help.
A She's gone out.
J I'm running low on everything.
A She'll be back in about an hour.
J I need some advice.
A Do you want me to take a message?
J No.
A She's gone to Tesco.
J
A She'll be back in about an hour.
J I'll stick tight.
A What's your name? My name's Angela.

Tuesday #3 19:07 (30 Secs)

A   It's now 7 minutes past 7. If you've just joined us welcome to the Al Blewitt show, we're taking requests right through 'til 9, playing all your favourite tunes and we've got a caller on Line 3. What's your name caller?

J   Hello CapCom, this is Ocean Rider.

A   And do you have a message for anyone out there tonight?

J   It's cold up here.

A   That's really beautiful. Andrew, if you're listening out there, Jo loves you very much.

J   I'm loosing power.

A   And do you have a request Jo?

J   I need a guidance report, urgently.

A   Well, we'll see what we can do and meanwhile, if there's anyone out there with a special message call us now on 0121 6333867.

Tuesday #4 22:30 (5 mins)

A   It's me. I'm in London.

J: Where've you been?

A   I just got on a train didn't I.

J   I don't care.

A   No I didn't pay. Oh God Becky its brilliant! You've got to come down.

J   That's it that's fine.

A   I've meet this bloke.

J   Are you talking to me?

A   Ed, oh he's really fantastic right, he's got this flat in Brixton, we're all staying there its really brilliant!

J   Are you listening?

A   You've got to come down.
J   Yes.
A   What are they saying?
J   What ever you say.
A   What did they say?
J   I don't care.
A   It's none of their business.
J   Al?
A   I don't care.
J   Bring me down.
A   I don't like it here.
J   I need to come home.
A   Can I come home?
J   Yes.
A   Please.
J   Of course.
A   I don't like anyone.
J   Al?
A   We've been waiting up.
J   Where've you been?
A   Can you come and get me?
J   And you can't bring me back.
A   I want to come back.
J   That's what you think.
A   Dad, we've run out of money can you send us
        thirty quid?
J   You're just a voice in my head now Al.
        I don't believe that's you.
        Al?
        Al?

Wednesday #1   17:15 (30 secs)

A   Caroline?

J   Al?

A   Yeah it's me. I just wondered…

J   Go ahead.

A   Can you come over?
         Only I've got something to tell you.

J   Go ahead.

A   No, it's important you've got to come over.

J   Yeh.

A   No, it's just really stupid that's all, really dumb.

J   Is that you Al?

A   I've taken a lot of pills Caroline.

J   What's your frequency?

A   About an hour ago, only, I don't feel so good
         now, will you come over?

J   Hello CapCom?

A   Only, I wish I hadn't done it now.

Saturday #1 16:10 (30 secs)

J   Check, check and check.

A   That's all readings on tables LR + B to D one
         hundred PC.

J   Check.

A   The code is 376L until we advise you otherwise.
         Stand by for further instructions.

J   How long now?

A   R minus 5 hours and forty seven minutes.
         How's it looking up there Jo?

J   Shaped like a ship Al.

A   Glad to hear it.

Saturday #2 18:54:30 (30 secs)

A   Okay?

J   Yeah.

A   Approaching R minus three hours and two minutes.

J   Check.

Saturday #3 20:50 (30 secs)

A   R minus sixty seven, that's six seven minutes.

J   Two more orbits, then I'm all yours Al.

A   Laps of honour Jo.

J   If you say so.

A   Hold her tight

J   I'm touching nothing without your say so Al.

A   It's going to be smooth.

Saturday #4 21:50 (10 mins)

A   Okay Frank's locked all the doors in here.
We've by-passed all the fuses to everything.
We're all set.
Are you still there Ocean Rider?

J   Roger.

A   You look great from down here Jo.
Everyone's very happy. All systems read as normal. The Uncle is happy, Bill's happy, we're all super relaxed down here.

J   Likewise Al. How long?

A   We have six minutes before the mark Jo. You're strapped in?

J   None tighter.

A   That's good. It's all looking good. We're all looking forward to seeing you again.

J   Waiting on instructions.

A   Stand by.

A   Bill says we're okay to detach part two from part
        one ready for return.
J   Go ahead.
A   Locks off.
J   Locks off.
A   Priming on.
J   Priming on.
A   Let her go.
J   She's gone.
A   R minus...six minutes. Nearly there.

J   I'll miss this Al.
A   We'll always have this Jo.

J   Ready to go local?
A   Ready to go local.
J   We're going local. Switching to manual fire.
A   Priming 6, 7 and 8.
J   That's set.
A   Looks like we're all set.
J   Ready to sweep up the pieces?
A   That won't be necessary Ocean Rider, she'll hold.
J   CapCom.
A   Jo.
J   Nothing.
A   Any messages.
J   No, I'll be home soon.
A   That's it.
        R minus two minutes.
        We're going to initiate firing. Mark 30 seconds
        and we're go.

	You have local and manual fire.
J	That's affirmative.
A	Standing by for a twenty second burst.
J	Standing by.
A	Fifteen. Let's make it a safe one.
	And Five, four, three, two, one, mark!
J	Twenty seconds.
A	Ten... and sixteen, seventeen, eighteen, nineteen twenty.
J	Boosters off.
A	And the fall has started.
J	Instrumentation says the fall is good. Navigation is green. There's no stopping me now Al. I'm coming home.
A	Roger Jo we're waiting on you.
J	There's going to be an extra shooting star tonight Al. You should get yourself outside watch me barrel on in.
A	Negative Jo, estimate 90, nine zero seconds till the radio whites out, I'm sticking with you.
J	Appreciated CapCom, we have cabin pressure holding at 5.5, E&I temperatures rising, all remaining systems remain go, we're falling fast Al. Hope they welded this one tight.
A	That's it Jo, I'm loosing you, speak to you in twenty. Welcome home.

Saturday #6 23:35 (30 secs)

A   Ocean Rider, this is CapCom do you copy?
         Ocean Rider, this is CapCom come in please.
         Ocean Rider, this is CapCom, please
         acknowledge.

Saturday #7 23:55 (30 secs)

A   Jo, this is Al, please acknowledge.
         This is CapCom calling Ocean Rider on
         107.6mhz, at twenty three fifty five, please
         acknowledge. Are you out there Jo?
         Jo?

SPACE STATION

For two days in July 2002 a new station appeared on the Metro Line in West Bromwich between Wednesbury and Wednesbury Parkway. Earth North Central was marked on all the maps in all the trains as a connecting station for the Moon and nearby planets.

On this new station three astronauts waited, in space suits with helmets and boxes, for their connecting Metro to take them off the planet and to complete their onward journey to Mars. After waiting on the platform for two days, reading newspapers, knitting, talking to the local youths, growing excited as every fresh train approached and disappointed as it passed by without stopping, the travellers were at last picked up by the Space Tram and left West Bromwich with a triumphant farewell speech from the local station's public address system ringing in their ears.

Notes for Midlands Metro

As part of Jubilee Arts' Platforms project, passengers travelling on the Birmingham-Wolverhampton Metro line will see that a new station has appeared, just beyond Wednesbury Parkway. This station, 'Earth North Central', is for the use of astronauts and other space travellers wishing to commute between West Bromwich and the rest of the solar system. Unfortunately, these routes are not covered by the Metro One Day Travel pass.

It's possible that passengers on the trams will have questions about the station particularly as we hope to alter the Metro maps on the trams to include the new station. They may ask Metro staff what's going on. If you wish to join in with our story we'd be delighted but please don't feel pressurised. If you want to play along with the project we suggest the following for starters (but only if you feel up for it):

Drivers: At the station before Earth North Central, following the recorded announcement on the trams telling passengers about the next stop, it would be fantastic if you announced on the manual system something like: 'this tram not stopping at Earth North Central'

Conductors: Just in case you are asked questions by the public, here is some information about the new 'service':

This is part of the integrated transport system that will hopefully eventually link up with the rest of the Milky Way. Cost of tickets: Off peak maximum £25,000 (sorry no Venusian Blats accepted).

Stops on the route: Mercury, Saturn, Mars, Jupiter, Venus, Neptune, Uranus, Pluto.

Regularity of Service: Pretty irregular at the moment to be honest but eventually the plan is for it to be one per hour.

Post: People can post cards into space from a postbox on Wednesbury Parkway Station or email them to space@stanscafe.co.uk. They are guaranteed a reply.

Have fun with it & thanks again,
Amanda, Sarah, Paula & James from Stan's Cafe.

Production Timetable
Wednesday 3rd July
11:00 - 17:00 On site north of Wednesbury Parkway
building platform: Amanda Hadingue, Sarah
Archdeacon, Paula Witig, Benny Semp, Jonny O'Hanlon,
James Yarker.

Thursday 4th July
Evening: In depot putting stickers on trains as they
         are withdrawn from service: Amanda Hadingue,
         Sarah Archdeacon, Paula Witig, James Yarker.

Friday 5th July
08:00 - 18:00 On site north of Wednesbury Parkway.
         Amanda Hadingue, Sarah Archdeacon, Paula
         Witig, James Yarker.

Saturday 6th July
08:00 - 19.30 On site north of Wednesbury Parkway.
         Amanda Hadingue, Sarah Archdeacon,
         Paula Witig, James Yarker.
12:00 - 19.30 Various locations. Ed Dimsdale (photos).
19:00 - 19:30 Metro Control Room Jonny O'Hanlon to
         play president's speech.
18:00 - 19.30 Wednesbury Parkway Emily Dawkes to act
         as steward.
19:00 - 19.30 On the train which is stopping to pick up
         the astronauts Benny Semp and James Yarker

Sunday 7th July
11:00 - 13:00 On site north of Wednesbury Parkway to
         remove station: Benny Semp, Jonny O'Hanlon,
         James Yarker.

Questions from *Space Station* commissioners with answers.

What role if any do you feel art has to play in society?

Evidence is all around us of art being used as the means to innumerable ends: commercial, political, educational, recreational, social and egotistical. All of these seem valid. Stan's Cafe has no didactic mission statement. Most of these motivations will influence our various projects in differing proportions. If forced to express a unifying drive behind our art maybe we would say it looks to promote the possibility of an alternative worldview.

We don't advocate any specific ideology but seek instead to enthuse people about the possibility of there being something else out there; something existing outside the market, outside sporting competition, outside consumerism, an alternative way of thinking. We make work that is a glimpse into some other world. This other world, which flickers between being an escape from and reflection of our own, is reinvented with every piece. It is ambiguous, open to interpretation, often funny, sometimes sad, dystopian, elegiac, ironic, passionate, mysterious and provocative. All of these seem valid.

How does your work challenge our use of public space?

Each new project is a formal and aesthetic puzzle to be solved. Before Platforms we hadn't seriously addressed the question of performing in public spaces. Our challenge was to make something that would work in this new context and remain distinctly 'Stan's Cafe'. How do we create a wormhole to other worlds in a place so starkly of this world?

We wanted *Space Station* to be a fleeting joke passed in the course of your day. The station was a means of making a close connection with audiences whilst retaining an otherworldly distance. The astronauts were an immediate image and yet inscrutable in their motives, a blank canvas for speculation and supposition. On reflection we were delighted that the most appropriate site for Earth North Central was the least prepossessing location, an open vista of brown-field Heart of England hinterland. Maybe this was a typical Stan's Cafe place, a place whose blankness became a virtue, beautiful if you look at it in the right kind of way.

Do you feel it is possible to gauge an audience's response to your work?

Of course, from inside the helmet you can see smiles and waves and when you are blanked. From Wednesbury Parkway you can overhear confusion and laughter and cynicism. You can read notes and emails of enquiry and support. We can gauge these responses but only in a gloriously un-empirical way, that's part of why it's so much fun.

The responses we miss are the latent thoughts, the long term memory, the musings and the low-grade folk history of these events. We miss the confusion, the questions and complications of people's responses. Has the psychogeography of that fragment of track been touched by our presence in any way at all? Does anyone still see

the ghost of Earth North Central as they pass that place?
These are the responses we will always miss, the ones we
want to invent a gauge for.

*What question would you have liked to have been asked?
And how would you respond?*

Would you like to make a piece for the Paris Metro?
Yes please.

About the illustration and design

The illustrations for the covers of these books were undertaken by students at Birmingham City University as the final module of their first-year illustration course during the Spring/Summer of 2018. The images were developed through workshops using variations of the theatre-devising methods employed by Stan's Cafe but adapted and applied to the making of visual work. The resulting work was shown in the pop-up exhibition *The Something Of Somebody Something* at Stan's Cafe's venue @AE Harris in May 2018.

The design concept of the books was produced by final year Graphic Design student Aimee Chapman. These were then further developed for print in a collaborative process between Stan's Cafe and the University's Innovation Product Support Service (IPSS) which involved helping the company to select appropriate DTP software, undertaking training and selecting a suitable print on demand service.

Gareth Courage
Lecturer in Illustration
Birmingham City University

www.ingramcontent.com/pod-product-compliance
Lightning Source LLC
Chambersburg PA
CBHW050628070726
47592CB00029B/2792